5-Minute Prayers

Around the
Advent
Wreath

Lisa M. Hendey

AVE MARIA PRESS AVE Notre Dame, Indiana

Nihil Obstat: Reverend Michael Heintz, PhD
             Censor Librorum
Imprimatur: Most Reverend Kevin C. Rhoades
             Bishop of Fort Wayne–South Bend
Given at: Fort Wayne, Indiana, May 4, 2022

Founded in 1865, Ave Maria Press is a ministry of the United States Province of Holy Cross.

www.avemariapress.com

Paperback: ISBN-13 978-1-64680-164-0

E-book: ISBN-13 978-1-64680-165-7

Cover image © ElenaMedvedeva / GettyImages.

Cover and text design by Samantha Watson.

Printed and bound in the United States of America.

Welcome!

Coming so quickly on the heels of Thanksgiving, Advent can be a shock to our senses. Beginning four Sundays before December 25, which sometimes means just three days after Thanksgiving, Advent calls us to live December differently than much of the world would have us do. Our churches look different, and the music, prayers, and scripture readings herald the start of something new. Our parish homes are awash in the purple and rose hues and sacred hymns of the season. At home, we gather our wreaths and search for our candles and try to shift to a pace that enables us to gather quietly together, in physical presence or perhaps remotely, for just a few minutes each day. While commerce tells us how many shopping days we have before Christmas, we who desire to fully live Advent mark these days in a different way. We count down not to the opening of presents but rather to the fulfillment of God's promises—yes, for each of us, but also for all humanity and, indeed, for all creation.

The Church instructs us on the nature and purpose of this holy season. Advent has a twofold character: preparation for the great Feast of Christmas, when we celebrate the coming of the Christ child at Bethlehem, and spiritual renewal as we anticipate Christ coming again in the fullness of time. In fact, the name *Advent* was derived from the Latin word *adventus*, meaning "coming" or "arrival." *Adventus* was a translation of the Greek word *parousia*, a term used in the New Testament pointing to the Second Coming of Christ. My hope and prayer is that this little booklet helps you and those with whom you share life and home to ready your hearts and minds for Christ being born anew.

For the past few years, we have collectively been plunged into a time of darkness, fear, and intense uncertainty. We continue to work our way through pandemic living and worldwide instability. Yet these months of loss and isolation have offered many of us time and mental space for introspection and stirred hopes for a brighter world. In some ways, the reset from our former ways of celebrating has reminded us to ponder what matters most in our lives, to lean into a trusting faith in God's presence, and to do what we can to love and connect with others. Being unable to be physically proximate to family and friends has deepened the love we feel for them and our longing for time together. Saying goodbye to loved ones who have passed away has rekindled our hope in the Communion of Saints. Forcing ourselves to stay home has reminded many of us of the beautiful potential of our own domestic churches as places of worship and prayer.

I love that Advent marks the beginning of our liturgical year. As an optimist and a planner, I always anticipate this season in the same way I look forward to setting annual resolutions each New Year's Day. As much as I love God and my Catholic faith, I am still always cognizant of my need to slow down, to rest in God's embrace, and to share the love I receive from God with others in my life. Advent invites me to reimagine all that remains to learn about what it means to be a true follower of Jesus Christ.

But Advent can rush past me before I know it! My days quickly fill up with many tasks and social gatherings, making it all too easy for me to miss what is most sacred about this time of year. Every moment seems occupied with readying my home and preparing my family's wonderful traditions. Frequently, in my haste to do it all and make lasting memories, I neglect to properly prepare my heart to celebrate the child Jesus, to make room for Christ in my life each day, and to set my soul on his coming in glory at the end of time.

The Advent Wreath

The custom of lighting and praying around Advent wreaths likely started with German Lutherans in the sixteenth century, but the precise history remains unclear. It's easy enough to create your own, and there are plentiful instructions available online showing you how to do so. The traditional materials are quite basic: four candles and evergreen branches set in a circle appropriately sized for a special prayer space in your home. Traditions vary on the colors of the four candles. Some places use four white candles, and others use red, but most common in the United States is one rose and three purple candles. Inexpensive taper candles work well, as do pillar candles or votive lights. Some people add ribbons or dried foliage for a bit more color. Use your creative skills to keep your wreath as simple or as fancy as you want.

The wreath's circle of evergreens represents the never-ending promise of eternal life. The purple candles (or perhaps white candles with purple ribbons) mark the solemn tone of the season and call us to wait patiently, eyes set on Christ. The rose candle (or white with rose ribbon) reminds us to rejoice as we draw near to Christmas. A single purple candle is lit each day of the first week of Advent and then two purple candles during the second week. The lighting of the rose candle is added for the third week, and all four candles are lit during the fourth week. The light of our Advent wreaths grows in the deepening darkness of late fall and early winter in the Northern Hemisphere, representing for us the Light of Christ that shines in the darkness of our broken and longing world. From the sacred spaces of our homes, Catholics and many other Christians await the celebration of our Messiah's birth.

Praying with This Booklet

There is no right way to use this booklet. If you live alone, perhaps you can gather with friends or family remotely, each lighting their own wreath or candles as you join for common prayer. Or perhaps your prayer and reflection might include journaling. If you live with other adults, adjust your reflection and conversation as best suits the needs of your household. If you are blessed with children in your home, involve them in whatever ways work for you. Young children will enjoy watching the lighting of candles, sitting in silence, listening to the scriptures, and perhaps even leading the prayer. Older children may most enjoy the few moments of stillness in their busy lives. Everyone ought to consider singing since, as St. Augustine is thought to have said, "The one who sings prays twice." The words for "O Come, O Come Emmanuel" are available for free download at https://www.avemariapress.com/products/5-minute-prayers-around-the-advent-wreath. There, you will also find short prayers to some of the saints whose feasts we celebrate during Advent.

When children are present, you may want to skip the written reflection that follows the short Bible reading each day and instead let the simple ritual actions of gathering, lighting candles, praying, singing, and listening to the Bible reading be your focus. Ask the children what they think about Advent, the short rituals, and the Bible reading or what they want to say to Jesus. Share your own thoughts. Faith sharing is not about right and wrong answers; it is about telling one another what we believe, wonder, or love about God. Sometimes it's mostly about the questions children have. If you don't have ready answers, talk about how you might find them, and then do so later on.

From December 17 through December 23, we pray the O Antiphons, which are drawn from Evening Prayer (from the Church's Liturgy of the Hours) for these days. Each antiphon celebrates a title of Christ and appears in this booklet at the beginning of the devotions for the appropriate day.

I pray that this little booklet can be for your family or your household a doorway into the profound solace of a well-kept Advent. With a few minutes of daily silence, scripture, prayer, private reflection or shared conversation, and maybe just a bit of singing, I hope you find and grow to cherish a place of quiet refuge around your Advent wreath. Put away any stressful expectations of what you think Advent should be, and allow this to be a time of simplicity, focus, and sacred longing for what matters most. May this season of great hope draw your hearts and minds closer to Christ and to others in the radiant light of God's amazing love!

First Sunday of Advent

Light the first purple candle and pray:

**Behold, the Lord will come,
and all his holy ones with him;
and on that day there will be a great light!**

Pray in silence or sing a verse of "O Come, O Come Emmanuel."

Read:
Jesus said to his disciples:
So will it be [also] at the coming of the Son of Man.
Two men will be out in the field;
one will be taken, and one will be left.
Two women will be grinding at the mill;
one will be taken, and one will be left.
Therefore, stay awake!
For you do not know on which day your Lord will come.

—Matthew 24:39b–42

Today marks a new beginning and an urgent call to a powerful mission. The signs of this holy season invite us to live vigilantly, set apart from what we may be experiencing in the world around us. We light the first of four candles, offering a tiny flicker of light that will burn ever more brightly throughout Advent. Songs of anticipation evoke the hope we feel. The color purple reminds us to live with penitent hearts, readying ourselves for a moment that will come unexpectedly. Christ's Second Coming will happen according to God's design, not by our plans. Jesus reminds us to be ready for him. With no certain itinerary but a clear destination, we move ahead with expectant hope, confident that God is with us every step of the way. Come, Lord Jesus!

In silence, journaling, or conversation, ask:
Where have I met Christ today?

Where will I watch for Christ tomorrow?

Pray:
Loving God, thank you for the gifts, blessings, and joys of this day. Accompany and strengthen us so that we may actively live your love among our neighbors. Amen.

While making the Sign of the Cross, pray together:
Come, Lord Jesus; come quickly!

First Monday of Advent

Light the first purple candle and pray:

**Behold, the Lord will come,
and all his holy ones with him;
and on that day there will be a great light!**

Pray in silence or sing a verse of "O Come, O Come Emmanuel."

Read:

"Come, let us climb the LORD's mountain,
    to the house of the God of Jacob,
That he may instruct us in his ways,
    and we may walk in his paths."
For from Zion shall go forth instruction,
    and the word of the LORD from Jerusalem.
He shall judge between the nations,
    and set terms for many peoples.
They shall beat their swords into plowshares
    and their spears into pruning hooks;
One nation shall not raise the sword against another,
    nor shall they train for war again.
House of Jacob, come,
    let us walk in the light of the LORD!

—Isaiah 2:3–5

This Advent, here in the shelter of our home, we begin a journey. God asks us to walk toward the peace and love of the Christmas promise. Our world is too often torn apart by sorrow, intolerance, violence, and deep injustices. But we need not fear, even in the darkness, because we are not climbing God's mountain alone. By reading God's Word, praying together, and lovingly supporting one another, we find the right path. Walking in the light means not only learning to better love God and our families but also carrying that love out into the world around us. Let's think about this together.

In silence, journaling, or conversation, ask:
Where have I met Christ today?

Where will I watch for Christ tomorrow?

Pray:
Loving God, thank you for the gifts, blessings, and joys of this day. Accompany and strengthen us so that we may actively live your love among our neighbors. Amen.

While making the Sign of the Cross, pray together:
Come, Lord Jesus; come quickly!

First Tuesday of Advent

Light the first purple candle and pray:

**Behold, the Lord will come,
and all his holy ones with him;
and on that day there will be a great light!**

Pray in silence or sing a verse of "O Come, O Come Emmanuel."

Read:

O God, give your judgment to the king;
    your justice to the king's son;
That he may govern your people with justice,
    your oppressed with right judgment.
That abundance may flourish in his days,
    great bounty, till the moon be no more.
May he rule from sea to sea,
    from the river to the ends of the earth.
For he rescues the poor when they cry out,
    the oppressed who have no one to help.
He shows pity to the needy and the poor
    and saves the lives of the poor.
May his name be blessed forever;
    as long as the sun, may his name endure.
May the tribes of the earth give blessings with his name;
    may all the nations regard him as favored.

—Psalm 72 1–2, 7–8, 12–13, 17

The words of the psalmist, although written millennia ago, still ring true in the hearts of God's faithful who yearn even now for an age when justice and peace will reign across the earth. During the quiet of this Advent season, as we gather in the light of our wreath, let us remember our neighbors who go unheard, unserved, and unloved. For so many, justice is withheld by systems and persons that fail to recognize the basic human dignity of every human life. In our waiting and watching today, let's examine how we might be inspired by God's love to bring compassion, healing, and abiding peace through humble acts of purposeful giving.

In silence, journaling, or conversation, ask:
Where have I met Christ today?

Where will I watch for Christ tomorrow?

Pray:
Loving God, thank you for the gifts, blessings, and joys of this day. Accompany and strengthen us so that we may actively live your love among our neighbors. Amen.

While making the Sign of the Cross, pray together:
Come, Lord Jesus; come quickly!

First Wednesday of Advent

Light the first purple candle and pray:

**Behold, the Lord will come,
and all his holy ones with him;
and on that day there will be a great light!**

Pray in silence or sing a verse of "O Come, O Come Emmanuel."

Read:
Jesus summoned his disciples and said,
"My heart is moved with pity for the crowd,
for they have been with me now for three days
and have nothing to eat.
I do not want to send them away hungry,
for fear they may collapse on the way."
The disciples said to him,
"Where could we ever get enough bread in this deserted place
to satisfy such a crowd?"
Jesus said to them, "How many loaves do you have?"
"Seven," they replied, "and a few fish."
He ordered the crowd to sit down on the ground.
Then he took the seven loaves and the fish,
gave thanks, broke the loaves, and gave them to the disciples,
who in turn gave them to the crowds. They all ate and were
   satisfied.
They picked up the fragments left over—seven baskets full.
—Matthew 15:32–37

This story about Jesus taking simple gifts of bread and fish and feeding thousands reminds us to stop, see, and respond to the needs of others. When we feel overwhelmed by all the world's problems, let's trust that we can go to God in our moments of need, but also remember that we are called to provide for one another. Transformed by Christ dwelling with us, we become a holy gift to others. How can we allow Christ to work in and through us to help friends in need?

In silence, journaling, or conversation, ask:
Where have I met Christ today?

Where will I watch for Christ tomorrow?

Pray:
Loving God, thank you for the gifts, blessings, and joys of this day. Accompany and strengthen us so that we may actively live your love among our neighbors. Amen.

While making the Sign of the Cross, pray together:
Come, Lord Jesus; come quickly!

First Thursday of Advent

Light the first purple candle and pray:

**Behold, the Lord will come,
and all his holy ones with him;
and on that day there will be a great light!**

Pray in silence or sing a verse of "O Come, O Come Emmanuel."

Read:
Jesus said to his disciples:
"Everyone who listens to these words of mine and acts on them
will be like a wise man who built his house on rock.
The rain fell, the floods came,
and the winds blew and buffeted the house.
But it did not collapse; it had been set solidly on rock.
And everyone who listens to these words of mine
but does not act on them
will be like a fool who built his house on sand.
The rain fell, the floods came,
and the winds blew and buffeted the house.
And it collapsed and was completely ruined."

—*Matthew 7:24–27*

Today, we commit to building the house of our faith on solid rock. It will stand the test of time and become a strong and lasting shelter for all who come to us in need. When they knock on the door, will we be ready to meet them with love and help them with their emotional, physical, and spiritual needs? As we await Jesus's coming, let us build upon the foundation given us by listening to God's Word and allowing it to transform our hearts.

In silence, journaling, or conversation, ask:
Where have I met Christ today?

Where will I watch for Christ tomorrow?

Pray:
Loving God, thank you for the gifts, blessings, and joys of this day. Accompany and strengthen us so that we may actively live your love among our neighbors. Amen.

While making the Sign of the Cross, pray together:
Come, Lord Jesus; come quickly!

First Friday of Advent

Light the first purple candle and pray:

**Behold, the Lord will come,
and all his holy ones with him;
and on that day there will be a great light!**

Pray in silence or sing a verse of "O Come, O Come Emmanuel."

Read:
One thing I ask of the LORD;
    this I seek:
To dwell in the LORD's house
    all the days of my life,
To gaze on the LORD's beauty,
    to visit his temple.
I believe I shall see the LORD's goodness
    in the land of the living.
Wait for the LORD, take courage;
    be stouthearted, wait for the LORD!

—Psalm 27:4, 13–14

When preaching on this psalm passage in 2004, St. John Paul II said that coming into God's true presence was "like coming into an oasis of light and love." How can we challenge ourselves to see the loveliness of God's existence in the world around us? Perhaps we recognize that beauty in the eyes of our children, in a sublime sunrise, or in the strains of our favorite Christmas carol. As we wait patiently, let's make an extra effort to notice and be grateful for every moment of grace.

In silence, journaling, or conversation, ask:
Where have I met Christ today?

Where will I watch for Christ tomorrow?

Pray:
Loving God, thank you for the gifts, blessings, and joys of this day. Accompany and strengthen us so that we may actively live your love among our neighbors. Amen.

While making the Sign of the Cross, pray together:
Come, Lord Jesus; come quickly!

First Saturday of Advent

Light the first purple candle and pray:

**Behold, the Lord will come,
and all his holy ones with him;
and on that day there will be a great light!**

Pray in silence or sing a verse of "O Come, O Come Emmanuel."

Read:
Jesus went around to all the towns and villages,
teaching in their synagogues,
proclaiming the gospel of the kingdom,
and curing every disease and illness.
At the sight of the crowds, his heart was moved with pity for
    them
because they were troubled and abandoned,
like sheep without a shepherd.
Then he said to his disciples,
"The harvest is abundant but the laborers are few;
so ask the master of the harvest
to send out laborers for his harvest."
Jesus sent out these twelve after instructing them thus,
"Go . . . to the lost sheep of the house of Israel.
As you go, make this proclamation: 'The kingdom of heaven
    is at hand.'
Cure the sick, raise the dead,
cleanse lepers, drive out demons.
Without cost you have received; without cost you are to give."
                    —Matthew 9:35–38; 10:5a, 6–8

Have you ever found yourself around a herd of sheep? It's an experience that engages all the senses! When a shepherd or his herding dog comes into their presence, suddenly this loud and smelly cacophony of animals becomes an organized force of nature, moving toward a common goal—usually getting to the food. In today's reading, Jesus likened the crowds following him to lost sheep, pointing to their need to be cared for. He then appointed his disciples as their shepherds, instructing them to feed the people spiritually. You and I play both roles in this story: we are sometimes the sheep and sometimes the shepherds. This Advent, we move alongside other sheep, trusting the protection of Jesus, the Good Shepherd. But we are also called to care for one another as shepherds do! No matter how old we are, we all have ways of giving to one another.

In silence, journaling, or conversation, ask:
Where have I met Christ today?

Where will I watch for Christ tomorrow?

Pray:
Loving God, thank you for the gifts, blessings, and joys of this day. Accompany and strengthen us so that we may actively live your love among our neighbors. Amen.

While making the Sign of the Cross, pray together:
Come, Lord Jesus; come quickly!

Second Sunday of Advent

Light the first two purple candles and pray:

**Hear the word of the Lord, O nations;
declare it to the distant lands:
Behold, our Savior will come; you need no longer fear!**

Pray in silence or sing a verse of "O Come, O Come Emmanuel."

Read:

A voice proclaims:

In the wilderness prepare the way of the LORD!

Make straight in the wasteland a highway for our God!

Every valley shall be lifted up,

every mountain and hill made low;

The rugged land shall be a plain,

the rough country, a broad valley.

Then the glory of the LORD shall be revealed,

and all flesh shall see it together;

for the mouth of the LORD has spoken.

Go up onto a high mountain,

Zion, herald of good news!

Cry out at the top of your voice,

Jerusalem, herald of good news!

—Isaiah 40:3–5, 9a

Have you ever set off on a journey, plugged your destination into your navigation tool, and been given a set of directions that surprised you? Sometimes the best path is not the most direct one. Today, Isaiah calls us to "prepare the way" for Jesus, to "make straight" a highway for our God. But life is messy, filled with unanticipated twists and turns. We wander, sometimes along wrong paths, longing for physical sustenance and spiritual consolation. Isaiah and John the Baptist encouraged their followers to make reparations in advance of Christ's coming. In what ways do we need to prepare our hearts this season so that Jesus will find a warm welcome in us? What way will we take to find Jesus?

In silence, journaling, or conversation, ask:
Where have I met Christ today?

Where will I watch for Christ tomorrow?

Pray:
Loving God, thank you for the gifts, blessings, and joys of this day. Accompany and strengthen us so that we may actively live your love among our neighbors. Amen.

While making the Sign of the Cross, pray together:
Come, Lord Jesus; come quickly!

Second Monday of Advent

Hear the word of the Lord, O nations;
declare it to the distant lands:
Behold, our Savior will come; you need no longer fear!

Pray in silence or sing a verse of "O Come, O Come Emmanuel."

Read:

One day as Jesus was teaching,

Pharisees and teachers of the law were sitting there

who had come from every village of Galilee and Judea and
Jerusalem,

and the power of the Lord was with him for healing.

And some men brought on a stretcher a man who was
paralyzed;

they were trying to bring him in and set [him] in his presence.

But not finding a way to bring him in because of the crowd,

they went up on the roof and lowered him on the stretcher

through the tiles into the middle in front of Jesus.

When he saw their faith, he said,

"As for you, your sins are forgiven."

—Luke 5:17–20

Have you ever wanted something so badly that you would do
anything to get it? Some of us might think automatically of a
favorite toy or gadget at the top of our wish list and remember
the long hours we stood in line for the privilege of buying

that item. For some of the men in today's gospel, the thing they wanted so greatly was the physical healing of their loved one. They wanted this so badly and trusted Jesus so intensely that they went to the roof of a home where he was staying and lowered the ill person into Jesus's presence. That is faith! Today as we remember our friends and loved ones who have asked for our prayers, let us approach God with faith that all will be well according to God's perfect plan. God knows and answers our prayers.

In silence, journaling, or conversation, ask:
Where have I met Christ today?

Where will I watch for Christ tomorrow?

Pray:
Loving God, thank you for the gifts, blessings, and joys of this day. Accompany and strengthen us so that we may actively live your love among our neighbors. Amen.

While making the Sign of the Cross, pray together:
Come, Lord Jesus; come quickly!

Second Tuesday of Advent

Light the first two purple candles and pray:

**Hear the word of the Lord, O nations;
declare it to the distant lands:
Behold, our Savior will come; you need no longer fear!**

Pray in silence or sing a verse of "O Come, O Come Emmanuel."

Read:
Go up onto a high mountain,
    Zion, herald of good news!
Cry out at the top of your voice,
    Jerusalem, herald of good news!
Cry out, do not fear!
    Say to the cities of Judah:
    Here is your God!
Here comes with power
    the Lord God,
    who rules by his strong arm;
Here is his reward with him,
    his recompense before him.
Like a shepherd he feeds his flock;
    in his arms he gathers the lambs,
Carrying them in his bosom,
    leading the ewes with care.

—Isaiah 40:9–11

Imagine, for just a moment, experiencing the happiest news you've ever heard. Overflowing with excitement, you climb to the peak of a tall mountain and proclaim your excitement for all to hear. Your words bounce from the rocks and echo across the valleys, inviting others to join in your celebration. Isaiah's prophecy today is both tender and titanic. Too major for him to keep to himself, his certain knowledge of the Messiah's coming is for all the world to hear. How can we participate in Isaiah's proclamation of the best news ever known to mankind? With the imagery and symbolism of Christmas proliferating around us, let's look today for tender ways to remind our friends and loved ones of the Shepherd's approach, even as we seek ways to shelter those in our flock who are most in need of care and protection.

In silence, journaling, or conversation, ask:
Where have I met Christ today?

Where will I watch for Christ tomorrow?

Pray:
Loving God, thank you for the gifts, blessings, and joys of this day. Accompany and strengthen us so that we may actively live your love among our neighbors. Amen.

While making the Sign of the Cross, pray together:
Come, Lord Jesus; come quickly!

Second Wednesday of Advent

Light the first two purple candles and pray:

Hear the word of the Lord, O nations;
declare it to the distant lands:
Behold, our Savior will come; you need no longer fear!

Pray in silence or sing a verse of "O Come, O Come Emmanuel."

Read:
Jesus said to the crowds:
"Come to me, all you who labor and are burdened,
and I will give you rest.
Take my yoke upon you and learn from me,
for I am meek and humble of heart;
and you will find rest for yourselves.
For my yoke is easy, and my burden light."

—*Matthew 11:28–30*

How overwhelmed we feel these days! Work and school
deadlines, the expectations of the holidays done right, and
the continual race of everyday life can wear us down to the
point of physical and spiritual exhaustion. Add to this financial
pressures, health concerns, and a daily news cycle that bears
far too much negativity, and we can feel at our limit. Today,
Jesus extends his arms to embrace all our *stuff*—the stuff that
depresses us, frightens us, and drags us into despair. His words
to the crowds, "*Come to me,*" beckon us to trust his embrace.
The light of the Advent candles represents the hope we have

in the One who is never too busy to carry us when we are at our weakest. Into his arms, we cast our burdens. Unyoked by the meekness and humility of Christ's love, we are set free.

In silence, journaling, or conversation, ask:
Where have I met Christ today?

Where will I watch for Christ tomorrow?

Pray:
Loving God, thank you for the gifts, blessings, and joys of this day. Accompany and strengthen us so that we may actively live your love among our neighbors. Amen.

While making the Sign of the Cross, pray together:
Come, Lord Jesus; come quickly!

Second Thursday of Advent

Light the first two purple candles and pray:

**Hear the word of the Lord, O nations;
declare it to the distant lands:
Behold, our Savior will come; you need no longer fear!**

Pray in silence or sing a verse of "O Come, O Come Emmanuel."

Read:

I will extol you, my God and king;
    I will bless your name forever and ever.
The LORD is good to all
    compassionate toward all your works.
All your works give you thanks, LORD,
    and your faithful bless you.
They speak of the glory of your reign
    and tell of your mighty works,
Making known to the sons of men your mighty acts,
    the majestic glory of your rule.
Your reign is a reign for all ages,
    your dominion for all generations.

—Psalm 145:1, 9–13a

"*Don't forget to say thank you.*" This lesson from my parents was one gift I hoped to pass along to my own children. Too often, we remember to *ask* when we have needs but neglect to *express gratitude* when they are met. Today's psalm calls us to reflect upon the good God has done in our lives and to testify to those blessings, sharing them with others. This feels easy when all goes according to our plans, but more challenging when real life is hard. Today, as we pause around our wreath, let us thank God for his steadfast presence in one difficult aspect of our Advent journey: an illness, a hardship, an isolation. We give thanks for the light of Christ, which seems to shine even more brightly in the darkness when we gather close, notice, and give praise.

In silence, journaling, or conversation, ask:
Where have I met Christ today?

Where will I watch for Christ tomorrow?

Pray:
Loving God, thank you for the gifts, blessings, and joys of this day. Accompany and strengthen us so that we may actively live your love among our neighbors. Amen.

While making the Sign of the Cross, pray together:
Come, Lord Jesus; come quickly!

Second Friday of Advent

Light the first two purple candles and pray:

**Hear the word of the Lord, O nations;
declare it to the distant lands:
Behold, our Savior will come; you need no longer fear!**

Pray in silence or sing a verse of "O Come, O Come Emmanuel."

Read:
Thus says the Lord, your redeemer,
    the Holy One of Israel:
I am the Lord, your God,
    teaching you how to prevail,
    leading you on the way you should go.
If only you would attend to my commandments,
    your peace would be like a river,
    your vindication like the waves of the sea,
Your descendants like the sand,
    the offspring of your loins like its grains,
Their name never cut off
    or blotted out from my presence.

—Isaiah 48:17–19

Jesus came to save us. Along the way to his ultimate act of life-giving, salvific love, he taught with words but also with quiet actions. He sought out the company of those considered unworthy. He made time for the childlike. He shared his miraculous gifts with outsiders. So often, we follow God's commandments within a false framework that excludes our loving notice of those most in need. In our desire to be "holy," we may turn our backs on those who might never know the richness of God's love unless we go out of our way to bring it to them. How can we choose today to follow the path God leads us along, which includes noticing those who may challenge our comfort levels? God's blessings, even more bountiful than the grains of sand or the blades of grass or the stars of the universe, are extended to all. We listen and learn so that we may share.

In silence, journaling, or conversation, ask:
Where have I met Christ today?

Where will I watch for Christ tomorrow?

Pray:
Loving God, thank you for the gifts, blessings, and joys of this day. Accompany and strengthen us so that we may actively live your love among our neighbors. Amen.

While making the Sign of the Cross, pray together:
Come, Lord Jesus; come quickly!

Second Saturday of Advent

**Hear the word of the Lord, O nations;
declare it to the distant lands:
Behold, our Savior will come; you need no longer fear!**

Pray in silence or sing a verse of "O Come, O Come Emmanuel."

Read:

Like fire a prophet appeared,
    his words a flaming furnace.
The staff of life, their bread, he shattered,
    and in his zeal he made them few in number.
By God's word he shut up the heavens
    and three times brought down fire.
How awesome are you, ELIJAH!
        Whose glory is equal to yours?
You were taken aloft in a whirlwind,
    in a chariot with fiery horses.
You were destined, it is written, in time to come
    to put an end to wrath before the day of the LORD,
To turn back the hearts of parents toward their children,
    and to re-establish the tribes of Jacob.
Blessed is the one who shall have seen you before he dies!
                —Sirach 48:1–4, 9–11

Today's scripture passage from Sirach is filled with imagery
that's far from the contemporary images of Christmas that

surround us. Instead of elves and snowmen, we read of the prophet Elijah whose prophecies were so potent that they are described as being like fire. Elijah and the other prophets who preceded Christ's coming taught their followers with an urgency that is often lacking in today's world. Even as people of faith, we may find ourselves stressed by all the things we think we need to do and to accomplish before Christmas. But do these items that press on us really matter in our quest to know and love God? Today, let's seek ways to see God's powerful goodness and love in the world around us. When we rest our heads for bed tonight, let's take a moment to fall asleep in God's friendship, glorifying him for all the blessings of this today.

In silence, journaling, or conversation, ask:
Where have I met Christ today?

Where will I watch for Christ tomorrow?

Pray:
Loving God, thank you for the gifts, blessings, and joys of this day. Accompany and strengthen us so that we may actively live your love among our neighbors. Amen.

While making the Sign of the Cross, pray together:
Come, Lord Jesus; come quickly!

Third Sunday of Advent

Light two purple candles and the pink one; then pray:

**Rejoice in the Lord always; again I say, rejoice.
Indeed, the Lord is near!**

Pray in silence or sing a verse of "O Come, O Come Emmanuel."

Read:
Rejoice in the Lord always.
I shall say it again: rejoice!
Your kindness should be known to all.
The Lord is near.
Have no anxiety at all, but in everything,
by prayer and petition, with thanksgiving,
make your requests known to God.
Then the peace of God that surpasses all understanding
will guard your hearts and minds in Christ Jesus.

—Philippians 4:4–7

As a child, I led my siblings in a time-honored tradition as the annual Christmas arrival of our maternal grandparents from Indiana drew near. We kids would sit on the curb, eagerly waiting for Grandma and Grandpa to drive up. Meanwhile, Mom worked frantically inside as we waited. It's only now as a mom myself that I recognize my mom's part of that tradition, which likely involved lots of last-minute cleaning. I simply knew the joy: they would come soon, and so would Christmas! The mood of our Advent preparations changes today with the lighting of the rose-colored candle on our Advent wreath. "Rejoice in the Lord always," Paul teaches us, asking us to set aside the anxieties that may keep us from knowing God's grace in our lives. How can we be more childlike in our joy at the coming of Jesus? Today, we remember to let God's peace and love help us bear any weight we feel. The Lord is near! He'll be here soon!

In silence, journaling, or conversation, ask:
Where have I met Christ today?

Where will I watch for Christ tomorrow?

Pray:
Loving God, thank you for the gifts, blessings, and joys of this day. Accompany and strengthen us so that we may actively live your love among our neighbors. Amen.

While making the Sign of the Cross, pray together:
Come, Lord Jesus; come quickly!

Third Monday of Advent

Light two purple candles and the pink one; then pray:

**Rejoice in the Lord always; again I say, rejoice.
Indeed, the Lord is near!**

Pray in silence or sing a verse of "O Come, O Come Emmanuel."

Read:

The oracle of one who hears what God says,
and knows what the Most High knows,
Of one who sees what the Almighty sees,
in rapture and with eyes unveiled:
How pleasant are your tents, Jacob;
your encampments, Israel!
Like palm trees spread out,
like gardens beside a river,
Like aloes the Lord planted,
like cedars beside water;
Water will drip from their buckets,
their seed will have plentiful water;
Their king will rise higher than Agag
and their dominion will be exalted.
I see him, though not now;
I observe him, though not near:
A star shall advance from Jacob,
and a scepter shall rise from Israel.

—Numbers 24:4–7, 17a

To understand the significance of today's scripture passage, it seems important to understand that Balaam was prophesying at the behest of Balak, king of the Moabites and an enemy of the Israelites. Through the intervention of his oracle, he spoke words that testified not only to God's presence within Israel but also to the salvation for all peoples that would spring from their midst. The books of the Old Testament are filled with visionaries who foretold the coming of Christ. As we come closer to our celebration of the Nativity, what in our world points us to eternal truths about God's love and God's plans for us? Tonight, take a step outside and look upward at the heavens. The vastness of God's creation is a tangible reminder of the limitlessness of his love for each of us.

In silence, journaling, or conversation, ask:
Where have I met Christ today?

Where will I watch for Christ tomorrow?

Pray:
Loving God, thank you for the gifts, blessings, and joys of this day. Accompany and strengthen us so that we may actively live your love among our neighbors. Amen.

While making the Sign of the Cross, pray together:
Come, Lord Jesus; come quickly!

Third Tuesday of Advent

Light two purple candles and the pink one; then pray:

**Rejoice in the Lord always; again I say, rejoice.
Indeed, the Lord is near!**

Pray in silence or sing a verse of "O Come, O Come Emmanuel."

Read:
Jesus asked, "What is your opinion?
A man had two sons. He came to the first and said,
'Son, go out and work in the vineyard today.'
He said in reply, 'I will not,'
but afterwards he changed his mind and went.
The man came to the other son and gave the same order.
He said in reply, 'Yes, sir,' but did not go.
Which of the two did his father's will?"
They answered, "The first."

—Matthew 21:28–31a

As I was walking down the street one day, I passed a man who appeared disheveled and upset. As I approached, he loudly asked me for a quarter. Answering honestly, I told him that I didn't have any cash and wished him a good day. As I moved away, I heard him yell loudly after me, "Hey, old lady. You need to go to church!" His words hit me like a gut punch. I knew at that moment that I had not acted against God's will directly. But what the man said caused me to think about the many times that I publicly profess or write about my faith and yet act in ways that are counter to the love that Jesus came to teach us. As we contemplate today's parable, may we pray together for the grace to answer God's invitation with sincerity and love.

In silence, journaling, or conversation, ask:
Where have I met Christ today?

Where will I watch for Christ tomorrow?

Pray:
Loving God, thank you for the gifts, blessings, and joys of this day. Accompany and strengthen us so that we may actively live your love among our neighbors. Amen.

While making the Sign of the Cross, pray together:
Come, Lord Jesus; come quickly!

Third Wednesday of Advent

Light two purple candles and the pink one; then pray:

**Rejoice in the Lord always; again I say, rejoice.
Indeed, the Lord is near!**

Pray in silence or sing a verse of "O Come, O Come Emmanuel."

Read:

I am the LORD, there is no other;
    I form the light, and create the darkness,
I make weal and create woe;
    I, the LORD, do all these things.
Let justice descend, you heavens, like dew from above,
    like gentle rain let the clouds drop it down.
Let the earth open and salvation bud forth;
    let righteousness spring up with them!
    I, the LORD, have created this.
Turn to me and be safe,
    all you ends of the earth,
    for I am God; there is no other!

—Isaiah 45:6c–8, 22

In my home state of California, we greet a good rainstorm with thanksgiving, as a sign of grace amid our drought-ridden dryness. A material sign like rain gives weight to concepts that can be hard for us to understand. God exists, even if we cannot see him. Yet time marches forward, often bringing into our days moments of sorrow, despair, or darkness. How can we find consolation and peace in these moments? How might we offer kindness as a sign of God's love to others who are struggling? Advent calls us to prepare ourselves for Christ's coming. At the same time, it remains one of the most fertile seasons to act in ways that announce to others that God is the Lord, that God is present for each of us, and that God's care will never end.

In silence, journaling, or conversation, ask:
Where have I met Christ today?

Where will I watch for Christ tomorrow?

Pray:
Loving God, thank you for the gifts, blessings, and joys of this day. Accompany and strengthen us so that we may actively live your love among our neighbors. Amen.

While making the Sign of the Cross, pray together:
Come, Lord Jesus; come quickly!

Third Thursday of Advent

**Rejoice in the Lord always; again I say, rejoice.
Indeed, the Lord is near!**

Pray in silence or sing a verse of "O Come, O Come Emmanuel."

Read:

When the messengers of John the Baptist had left,
Jesus began to speak to the crowds about John.
"What did you go out to the desert to see—a reed swayed by
the wind?
Then what did you go out to see?
Someone dressed in fine garments?
Those who dress luxuriously and live sumptuously
are found in royal palaces.
Then what did you go out to see?
A prophet? Yes, I tell you, and more than a prophet.
This is the one about whom scripture says:
'Behold, I am sending my messenger ahead of you,
he will prepare your way before you.'
I tell you, among those born of women, no one is greater than
John;
yet the least in the kingdom of God is greater than he."
—*Luke 7:24–28.*

My favorite image of the Visitation of Mary to Elizabeth
was painted in 2008 by the artist James B. Janknegt. In this

contemporary icon, Janknegt depicts Jesus and John the Baptist nestled inside their mothers' wombs, but as men, not infants. John, garbed in crude animal pelts, rejoices with his arms aloft at the sight of Jesus, who wears a crown of gold atop his head and extends a sign of peace toward John. John's excitement at the recognition of the Messiah is clear from the image. He has given his life to making this news known. He cannot contain himself! This week, as the light of our rose candle reminds us to pray with joy, how can we live for Jesus as John did? Baptized in the light of Christ's love, we announce by our very lives God's light of hope for others.

In silence, journaling, or conversation, ask:
Where have I met Christ today?

Where will I watch for Christ tomorrow?

Pray:
Loving God, thank you for the gifts, blessings, and joys of this day. Accompany and strengthen us so that we may actively live your love among our neighbors. Amen.

While making the Sign of the Cross, pray together:
Come, Lord Jesus; come quickly!

Third Friday of Advent

Light two purple candles and the pink one; then pray:

**Rejoice in the Lord always; again I say, rejoice.
Indeed, the Lord is near!**

Pray in silence or sing a verse of "O Come, O Come Emmanuel."

Read:

May God be gracious to us and bless us;
    may his face shine upon us.
So shall your way be known upon the earth;
    your victory among all the nations.
May the nations be glad and rejoice;
    for you judge the peoples with fairness,
    you guide the nations upon the earth.
The earth has yielded its harvest;
    God, our God, blesses us.
May God bless us still,
    that the ends of the earth may revere him!

                      —Psalm 67:2–3, 5, 7–8

As we pray the words of today's psalm around our Advent wreath, now is a good time to remember our friends and family who will not be with us this year at Christmas. We pray for peace and union with God for those who have gone before us in death. We pray for our family members and loved ones who will spend this holiday serving others, for their safety and protection. We pray for all those around the world who will go without this Christmas: without food, without shelter, without the company of others. May they know God's love and presence, his nearness to them, even in their need. In recounting our blessings, how might we make this holiday season better for someone else? Today, let's also actively pray for the nations of our world to be united in peace and accord and for all in need of God's mercy.

In silence, journaling, or conversation, ask:
Where have I met Christ today?

Where will I watch for Christ tomorrow?

Pray:
Loving God, thank you for the gifts, blessings, and joys of this day. Accompany and strengthen us so that we may actively live your love among our neighbors. Amen.

While making the Sign of the Cross, pray together:
Come, Lord Jesus; come quickly!

Third Saturday of Advent or December 17

Light two purple candles and the pink one; then pray:

O Wisdom,
O Holy Word of God,
you govern all creation with
your strong yet tender care.
Come and show your people the way
to salvation.

Pray in silence or sing a verse of "O Come, O Come Emmanuel."

Read:

See, days are coming—oracle of the LORD—
    when I will raise up a righteous branch for David;
As king he shall reign and govern wisely,
    he shall do what is just and right in the land.
In his days Judah shall be saved,
    Israel shall dwell in security.
This is the name to be given him:
    "The LORD our justice."

—Jeremiah 23:5–8

I shared a conversation about healthy living with a friend. We agreed that, although we intellectually know the choices we should make, we sometimes knowingly walk down the wrong path. In today's O Antiphon, we pray, "Come and show your people the way to salvation." Surely, the prophet Jeremiah was pointing the people of his time to the way when he prophesied that a wise and righteous king would be raised up. We know that way is found through Jesus. But like the people of Jeremiah's time, we too often neglect or even willfully disregard the teachings we know will lead us to a path of salvation. For the remainder of Advent, how can we more thoroughly follow the way that God has shown us? The Lord, our God, is justice and light. May we always cling to the path that leads us home to him.

In silence, journaling, or conversation, ask:
Where have I met Christ today?

Where will I watch for Christ tomorrow?

Pray:
Loving God, thank you for the gifts, blessings, and joys of this day. Accompany and strengthen us so that we may actively live your love among our neighbors. Amen.

While making the Sign of the Cross, pray together:
Come, Lord Jesus; come quickly!

Fourth Sunday of Advent or December 18

Light all four candles and pray:

O Sacred Lord of ancient Israel,
who showed yourself to Moses in the burning bush,
who gave him the holy law on Sinai mountain:
Come, stretch out your mighty hand to set us free.

Pray in silence or sing a verse of "O Come, O Come Emmanuel."

Read:

When his mother Mary was betrothed to Joseph,
but before they lived together,
she was found with child through the holy Spirit.
Joseph her husband, since he was a righteous man,
yet unwilling to expose her to shame,
decided to divorce her quietly.
Such was his intention when, behold,
the angel of the Lord appeared to him in a dream and said,
"Joseph, son of David,
do not be afraid to take Mary your wife into your home.
For it is through the holy Spirit
that this child has been conceived in her.
She will bear a son and you are to name him Jesus,
because he will save his people from their sins."

—*Matthew 1:18b–21*

When reading a mystery novel, I often read the last chapter first. Trusting what is to come calms me and sets me free to focus on what is unfolding. In today's O Antiphon, we pray, "Come, stretch out your mighty hand to set us free," as we invite Jesus into our lives. For Joseph, who must have worried when he learned that Mary was pregnant, God sent the gift of an angel in a dream to encourage him. Joseph's faith gave him the freedom to say yes to what was unfolding in his life. Trust God to free you also from fear and worry.

In silence, journaling, or conversation, ask:
Where have I met Christ today?

Where will I watch for Christ tomorrow?

Pray:
Loving God, thank you for the gifts, blessings, and joys of this day. Accompany and strengthen us so that we may actively live your love among our neighbors. Amen.

While making the Sign of the Cross, pray together:
Come, Lord Jesus; come quickly!

Fourth Monday of Advent or December 19

Light all four candles and pray:

**O Root of Jesse's Stem,
you have been raised up as a sign for all peoples;
kings stand silent in your presence;
the nations bow down in worship before you.
Come, let nothing keep you from coming to our aid.**

Pray in silence or sing a verse of "O Come, O Come Emmanuel."

Read:

There was a certain man from Zorah, of the clan of the Danites,
whose name was Manoah.

His wife was barren and had borne no children.

An angel of the LORD appeared to the woman and said to her,

Though you are barren and have had no children,

you will conceive and bear a son.

The woman went and told her husband,

"A man of God came to me;

he had the appearance of an angel of God, fearsome indeed.

I did not ask him where he came from, nor did he tell me his
name.

But he said to me,

'You will conceive and will bear a son.

So drink no wine or beer, and eat nothing unclean.

For the boy shall be a nazirite for God from the womb,

until the day of his death.'"

The woman bore a son and named him Samson,
and when the boy grew up the LORD blessed him.
The Spirit of the LORD came upon him.

—Judges 13:2–3, 6–7, 24–25a

In today's O Antiphon, we ask Jesus, "Come, let nothing keep you from coming to our aid." Like Samson's mother, we have been offered a sign of God's passionate love for us: Jesus, the Christ, who has come to save us. In the busyness of these last days of Advent, pause to consider the signs of God's love all around you and invite him to come to fill your heart.

In silence, journaling, or conversation, ask:
Where have I met Christ today?

Where will I watch for Christ tomorrow?

Pray:
Loving God, thank you for the gifts, blessings, and joys of this day. Accompany and strengthen us so that we may actively live your love among our neighbors. Amen.

While making the Sign of the Cross, pray together:
Come, Lord Jesus; come quickly!

Fourth Tuesday of Advent or December 20

Light all four candles and pray:

**O Key of David,
O royal power of Israel,
controlling at your will the gate of heaven; come,
break down the prison walls of death
for those who dwell in darkness and the shadow of death;
and lead your captive people into freedom.**

Pray in silence or sing a verse of "O Come, O Come Emmanuel."

Read:
The LORD spoke to Ahaz:
Ask for a sign from the LORD, your God;
    let it be deep as Sheol, or high as the sky!
But Ahaz answered,
    "I will not ask! I will not tempt the LORD!"
Then he said:
    Listen, house of David!
Is it not enough that you weary human beings?
    Must you also weary my God?
Therefore the Lord himself will give you a sign;
    the young woman, pregnant and about to bear a son,
    shall name him Emmanuel.

—Isaiah 7:10–14

Today, we read that Isaiah was sent to King Ahaz to offer assurance. Ministering to Ahaz, the prophet spoke words of great hope, promising a Messiah. His very name, "Emmanuel" (meaning "God is with us"), was a sign that God would indeed be with them. In today's O Antiphon we pray to Jesus as "Key of David." How is faith a "key" that enables us to unlock peace and freedom? How can we share this key with others to reassure them that God is with us? Our loving presence, attention, help, or kindness toward one another serves as a sign that even in our hard times we are not alone.

In silence, journaling, or conversation, ask:
Where I have met Christ today?

Where will I watch for Christ tomorrow?

Pray:
Loving God, thank you for the gifts, blessings, and joys of this day. Accompany and strengthen us so that we may actively live your love among our neighbors. Amen.

While making the Sign of the Cross, pray together:
Come, Lord Jesus; come quickly!

Fourth Wednesday of Advent or December 21

Light all four candles and pray:

**O Radiant Dawn,
splendor of eternal light, sun of justice;
Come, shine on those who dwell in darkness.**

Pray in silence or sing a verse of "O Come, O Come Emmanuel."

Read:

During those days Mary set out
and traveled to the hill country in haste
to a town of Judah,
where she entered the house of Zechariah
and greeted Elizabeth.
When Elizabeth heard Mary's greeting,
the infant leaped in her womb,
and Elizabeth, filled with the holy Spirit,
cried out in a loud voice and said,
"Most blessed are you among women,
and blessed is the fruit of your womb.
And how does this happen to me,
that the mother of my Lord should come to me?
For at the moment the sound of your greeting reached my ears,
the infant in my womb leaped for joy.
Blessed are you who believed
that what was spoken to you by the Lord

would be fulfilled."

—*Luke 1:39–45*

I love to imagine what this greeting between Elizabeth and Mary was like. I can picture a long embrace, their joy at being together. Today, we invite Jesus, the Radiant Dawn, to come and shine upon those who dwell in darkness. How can we reclaim the radiance of Christ's presence to find comfort and peace? May the light of Christmas bring the same deep joy of knowing Jesus that Elizabeth knew immediately when greeting her cousin Mary.

In silence, journaling, or conversation, ask:
Where have I met Christ today?

Where will I watch for Christ tomorrow?

Pray:
Loving God, thank you for the gifts, blessings, and joys of this day. Accompany and strengthen us so that we may actively live your love among our neighbors. Amen.

While making the Sign of the Cross, pray together:
Come, Lord Jesus; come quickly!

Fourth Thursday of Advent or December 22

Light all four candles and pray:

O King of all nations and keystone of the Church: come and save us, whom you formed from the dust!

Pray in silence or sing a verse of "O Come, O Come Emmanuel."

Read:
"My soul proclaims the greatness of the Lord;
my spirit rejoices in God my savior.
For he has looked upon his handmaid's lowliness;
behold, from now on will all ages call me blessed.
The Mighty One has done great things for me,
and holy is his name.
His mercy is from age to age
to those who fear him.
He has shown might with his arm,
dispersed the arrogant of mind and heart.
He has thrown down the rulers from their thrones
but lifted up the lowly.
The hungry he has filled with good things;
the rich he has sent away empty.
He has helped Israel his servant,
    remembering his mercy,
according to his promise to our fathers,
    to Abraham and to his descendants forever."

—Luke 1:46–55

The night before my second son's birth was to be induced, my joy, but also my fear, overwhelmed me. With this memory, I think of young Mary, pregnant with Jesus, responding to the joy of Elizabeth's recognition of her situation. Surely, she was anxious about what her future would hold and about the well-being of the tiny child growing within her. But even engulfed in these feelings, Mary burst into prayer, glorifying God. As we near Christmas, how do our words and actions magnify the greatness of God working within us?

In silence, journaling, or conversation, ask:
Where have I met Christ today?

Where will I watch for Christ tomorrow?

Pray:
Loving God, thank you for the gifts, blessings, and joys of this day. Accompany and strengthen us so that we may actively live your love among our neighbors. Amen.

While making the Sign of the Cross, pray together:
Come, Lord Jesus; come quickly!

Fourth Friday of Advent
or December 23

Light all four candles and pray:

O Emmanuel,
King and Lawgiver,
Desire of nations, Savior of all peoples:
Come and set us free, Lord our God.

Pray in silence or sing a verse of "O Come, O Come Emmanuel."

Read:

Make known to me your ways, LORD;
    teach me your paths.
Guide me by your fidelity and teach me,
    for you are God my savior.
Good and upright is the LORD;
    therefore he shows sinners the way,
He guides the humble in righteousness,
    and teaches the humble his way.
All the paths of the LORD are mercy and truth
    toward those who honor his covenant and decrees.
The counsel of the LORD belongs to those who fear him;
    and his covenant instructs them.

—Psalm 25:4–5ab, 8–9, 10, 14

As I pen this reflection, I am sitting with my father, who rests in a long-term hospice bed with end-stage dementia. The part of me that desires control over my life's circumstances often bristles against the many unknowns of this path. Today's psalm, a reminder that God has made a covenant with each of us, challenges me to lean in, confident that God is with me always, guiding me even along sometimes dark paths. How has your Advent journey led you toward a deeper friendship with God? When the way ahead feels daunting, let's remember to humble ourselves, to seek God's friendship, and to allow ourselves to be led forward, strengthened by God's constant presence with us.

In silence, journaling, or conversation, ask:
Where have I met Christ today?

Where will I watch for Christ tomorrow?

Pray:
Loving God, thank you for the gifts, blessings, and joys of this day. Accompany and strengthen us so that we may actively live your love among our neighbors. Amen.

While making the Sign of the Cross, pray together:
Come, Lord Jesus; come quickly!

Fourth Saturday of Advent or Christmas Eve

Light all four candles and pray:

Behold, a Virgin shall conceive and bear a son; and his name will be called Emmanuel!

Pray in silence or sing a verse of "O Come, O Come Emmanuel."

Read:

"Blessed be the Lord, the God of Israel;

for he has visited and brought redemption to his people.

He has raised up a horn for our salvation,

within the house of David his servant,

even as he promised through the mouth of his holy prophets from of old:

salvation from our enemies and from the hand of all who hate us,

to show mercy to our fathers

and to be mindful of his holy covenant

and of the oath he swore to Abraham our father,

and to grant us that, rescued from the hand of enemies,

without fear we might worship him in holiness and righteousness, before him all our days.

And you, child, will be called prophet of the Most High,

for you will go before the Lord to prepare his ways,

to give his people knowledge of salvation

through the forgiveness of their sins,

because of the tender mercy of our God

by which the daybreak from on high shall visit us
to shine on those who sit in darkness and death's shadow,
to guide our feet into the path of peace."

—*Luke 1:68–79*

My brother Patrick starred as mute Zechariah, father of John the Baptist, in my family's Christmas pageant, holding a handwritten sign that read, "His name is John!" After Zechariah's obedient act ended a period of divine correction, Patrick was able to speak aloud, and we danced loudly, shouting, "Zechariah can speak! It's a miracle!" Zechariah's canticle of praise is meant for our ears too. We pause tonight to give praise before the manger, our Advent wreath aglow. May we, on this holy feast, welcome the Lord with open hearts and shouts of joy!

In silence, journaling, or conversation, ask:
Where have I met Christ today?

Where will I watch for Christ tomorrow?

Pray:
Loving God, thank you for the gifts, blessings, and joys of this day. Accompany and strengthen us so that we may actively live your love among our neighbors. Amen.

While making the Sign of the Cross, pray together:
Come, Lord Jesus; come quickly!

Lisa M. Hendey is the founder of the award-winning Catholic-Mom.com. She is the bestselling author of multiple books for adults and children, including *The Handbook for Catholic Moms*, *A Book of Saints for Catholic Moms*, *The Grace of Yes*, *I'm a Saint in the Making*, and the Chime Travelers fiction series.

Hendey has appeared on EWTN, on CatholicTV, and as a part of the Momnipotent DVD series. Her work has appeared in *Catholic Digest*, *National Catholic Register*, and *Our Sunday Visitor*.

Hendey travels internationally, giving workshops for adults and children. She has spoken at the Los Angeles Religious Education Congress, the Catholic Marketing Network, the University of Dallas Ministry Conference, the National Catholic Youth Conference, the Midwest Catholic Family Conference, and the National Council of Catholic Women. Selected as an Egan Journalism Fellow with Catholic Relief Services, Hendey has traveled, written, and spoken on behalf of CRS, Unbound, and other nonprofit organizations to support their humanitarian missions in Rwanda, the Philippines, India, Tanzania, Kenya, and Columbia.

She lives with her husband, Greg, in Los Angeles, California.

lisahendey.com
Facebook: lisamhendey
Twitter: @LisaHendey
Instagram: @lisahendey
Pinterest: lisahendey
YouTube: Lisa Hendey